D1560622

J
567.97
Sa
Sandell, Elizabeth J

on inv.

Maiasaura:  The Good Mother
Dinosaur

DATE DUE

| DATE DUE | | | |
|---|---|---|---|
| DEC. 09 2003 | | | |
| JUN. 0 2004 | | | |
| JAN 0 2006 | | | |
| SEP 0 0 2006 | | | |
| | | | |
| | | | |
| | | | |
| | | | |
| | | | |
| | | | |
| | | | |

11-98

Discard

Fulton Public Library
Fulton, Illinois

DEMCO

# MAIASAURA

## THE GOOD MOTHER DINOSAUR

by

## Elizabeth J. Sandell

DINOSAUR DISCOVERY ERA

**Bancroft-Sage Publishing**

601 Elkcam Circle, Suite C-7, Box 355, Marco, FL 33969

Exclusive distributor

ENCYCLOPAEDIA BRITANNICA EDUCATIONAL CORPORATION

TRAINING & DEVELOPMENT

310 South Michigan Avenue  Chicago. IL 60604

## LIBRARY OF CONGRESS CATALOGING IN PUBLICATION DATA

Sandell, Elizabeth J.
   Maiasaura: the good mother dinosaur.

   (Dinosaur discovery era)
   SUMMARY: Describes what is known about the recently discovered duckbilled dinosaur called Maiasaura, as suggested by current fossil evidence.
   1. Maiasaura--Juvenile literature. (1. Maiasaura. 2. Dinosaurs. 3. Paleontology.) I. Oelerich, Marjorie L. II. Hansen, Harlan S. III. Vista III Design. IV. Title. V. Series.
   QE862.O65S347    1989              567.9'7              88-39799
   ISBN 0-944280-17-X (lib. bdg.)
   ISBN 0-944280-23-4 (pbk bdg.)

| **International Standard Book Number:** | **Library of Congress Catalog Card Number:** |
|---|---|
| Library Binding 0-944280-17-X | 88-39799 |
| Paperback Binding 0-944280-23-4 | |

## SPECIAL THANKS FOR THEIR HELP AND COOPERATION TO:
Mary R. Carman, Paleontology Collection Manager
Field Museum of Natural History
Chicago, IL

Douglas Henderson, Paleoartist
Livingston, MT

John R. Horner, Ph.D.
Museum of the Rockies, Montana State University
Bozeman, MT

Copyright 1989 by Bancroft-Sage Publishing. All rights reserved. No part of this book may be reproduced in any form without written permission from the publisher, except for brief passages included in a review. Printed in the United States of America.

# MAIASAURA

## THE GOOD MOTHER DINOSAUR

**AUTHOR**

Elizabeth J. Sandell

dedicated to Danny

**EDITED BY**

Marjorie L. Oelerich, Ph.D.
Professor of Early Childhood and Elementary Education
Mankato State University
Mankato, MN

Harlan S. Hansen, Ph.D.
Professor of Early Childhood and Elementary Education
University of Minnesota
Minneapolis, MN

**ILLUSTRATED BY**

Vista III Design

**BANCROFT-SAGE PUBLISHING**
533 8th St. So., Box 664, Naples, FL 33939-0664 USA

# INTRODUCTION: RESTORING DINOSAURS

Mychal and his family went to visit the Museum of the Rockies in Bozeman, Montana (USA). The museum guide showed them into the exhibit hall. Here, they saw a man drawing pictures of the dinosaurs on display.

"This is Mr. Douglas Henderson," the museum guide told Mychal. "Mr. Henderson is a paleoartist."

"How is a paleoartist different from an artist?" Mychal asked Mr. Henderson.

"Well, Mychal," Mr. Henderson replied, "we only draw and paint pictures of plants and animals that lived many years ago. We also make models of what these plants and animals, such as dinosaurs, probably looked like. We try to show how dinosaurs lived and what they probably ate. All of this work is called 'restoring.'"

"How do you know what the dinosaurs really looked like?" Mychal asked.

"We work closely with paleontologists, who know a great deal about dinosaurs," Mr. Henderson explained. "These scientists collect information from the fossils of dinosaurs, including bones, teeth, skin, eggs, nests, and footprints."

"How do you decide the shape of the dinosaurs?" asked Mychal.

"We study animals we can see today, such as elephants, rhinoceroses, crocodiles, and ostriches. We look at how the bones in the body fit together. We also study how the muscles and skin go together to give shape to an animal," Mr. Henderson said.

"When we study dinosaur bones," he continued, "we can see rough spots, such as scars and ridges. These marks show where and how the muscles were attached to the bones. This helps us decide how the dinosaurs were shaped."

"It sounds like paleoartists must know a lot about an animal before they can draw it or make a model of it," said Mychal.

"You are right," Mr. Henderson replied. "We depend a great deal on the work of paleontologists, such as Dr. John Horner, who knows about dinosaurs. In our museum, the guide will show you skeletons of dinosaurs which Dr. Horner discovered."

So, the museum guide started Mychal and his family on a tour of the museum displays. The first exhibit was of a very special dinosaur, named *Maiasaura*.

"This *Maiasaura* skeleton was found by Dr. Horner," the museum guide explained. "He has found many dinosaur fossils. In fact, Dr. Horner found his first fossil bone when he was only seven years old.

"Let me tell you more about *Maiasaura* and how paleoartists 'restore' this dinosaur," the guide suggested.

# CHAPTER 1: FOSSILS OF MAIASAURA

Dr. John Horner found the very first fossils of *Maiasaura* (may ee uh sor´ uh) in 1978, in the mountains of Montana (USA). This was a kind of dinosaur which had never been found before. In the same area, Dr. Horner found fossil bones of baby dinosaurs as well as others which were older and bigger. He also found fossil nests and eggs of several other kinds of dinosaurs.

Dr. Horner and his friend, Robert Makela, were looking for fossils in Montana. They had been told that they might find a skeleton of a baby dinosaur in that area. They looked very carefully.

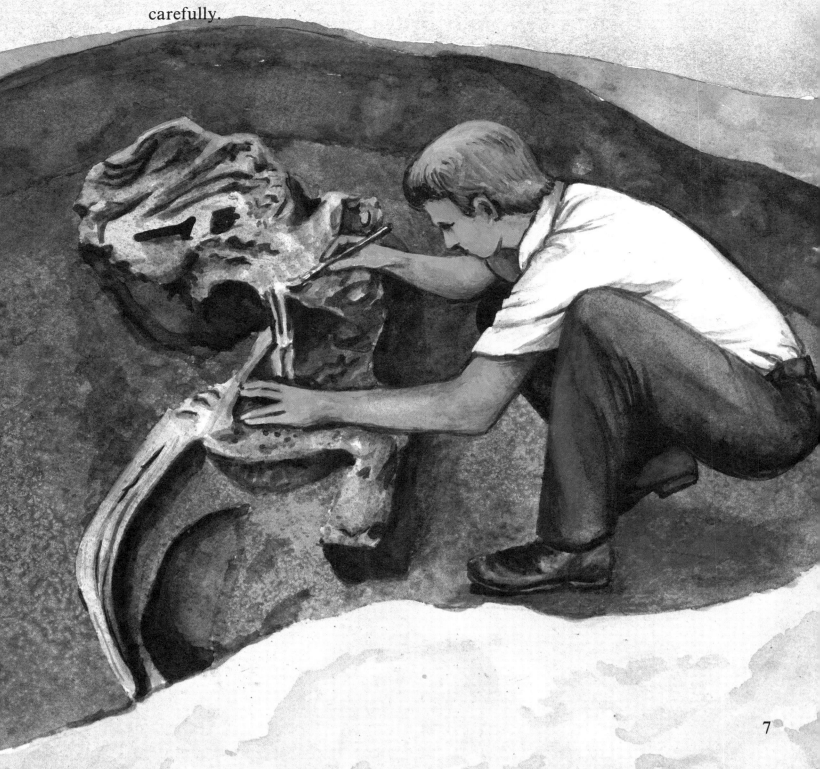

First, they found the bones of one baby dinosaur. Then, fossils of three more baby dinosaurs were discovered. Nearby, there were fossils of eleven more baby dinosaurs together in a nest.

The skull of an adult dinosaur was also discovered in the same area. It seemed like the adult dinosaur might have been in charge of all the nests and eggs. This reminded Dr. Horner of what a good mother might do. He wondered if this might have been a female dinosaur. If this were the mother, she would probably have been a good mother, because she guarded so many baby dinosaurs close together.

Dr. Horner, therefore, named this dinosaur *Maiasaura*, which means "good mother lizard." The Greek word **maia** for "good mother" was put together with the word **saura** for "lizard."

*Maiasaura* is spelled with an "a" instead of "us" at the end to make it mean a female animal. If this dinosaur would have been named for the male, Dr. Horner would have used the word *Maiasaurus*. Instead, *Maiasaura* is now used for the name of the males as well as the females of this particular dinosaur.

9

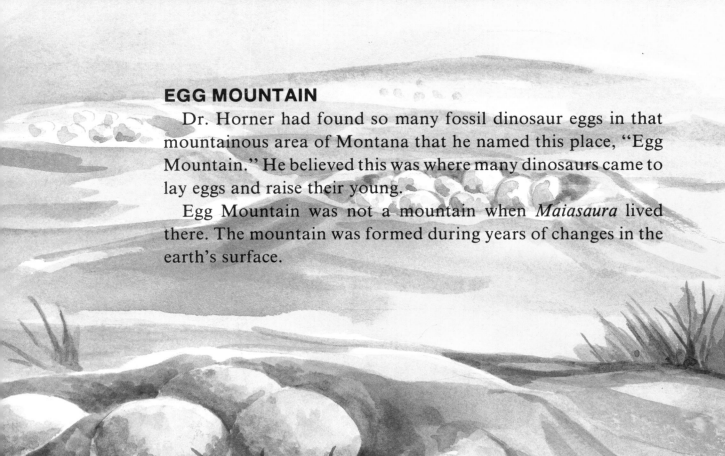

## EGG MOUNTAIN

Dr. Horner had found so many fossil dinosaur eggs in that mountainous area of Montana that he named this place, "Egg Mountain." He believed this was where many dinosaurs came to lay eggs and raise their young.

Egg Mountain was not a mountain when *Maiasaura* lived there. The mountain was formed during years of changes in the earth's surface.

## WEATHER AND PLANTS

When *Maiasaura* lived on earth, there were many shallow seas. The land was almost connected, like this map.

## LATE CRETACEOUS

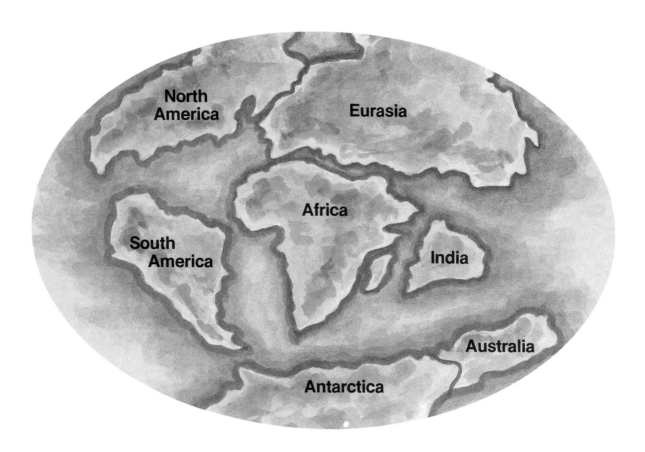

The weather may have been very mild when *Maiasaura* lived. The summers were warm and wet, and there were no cold winters.

*Maiasaura* lived in plains, swamps, hills, and forests. There were many trees, such as pine, cypress, palm, walnut, redwood, fig, and oak. There were flowering bushes, berry bushes, and leafy plants, such as magnolia. There were ferns and holly. Also, there were many butterflies and other insects.

## FOSSILS OF DINOSAURS

Earthquakes and volcanoes caused the land to change as it moved up and down. Some land rose up and became mountains. Other land became the bottom of rivers. Some of the rock where dinosaur fossils were buried was pushed to the top.

Fossils of *Maiasaura* were found in some of these layers of rock. Fossils were sometimes formed when a dinosaur died, and its body was covered with mud. The minerals from the mud would then turn the bones into fossils.

# CHAPTER 2: PALEOARTISTS SHOW HOW DINOSAURS LOOKED

Paleoartists examine fossils before they draw an animal skeleton on paper. They also learn about shapes and behaviors of animals with which we are familiar today. This information helps the paleoartist know what shape to give the dinosaur.

To draw pictures of *Maiasaura*, the paleoartist would first need to know that this animal was from a group of dinosaurs which were called *hadrosaurids* (had´ ruh sor´ ids). Scientists used the Greek words **hadros**, which means "bulky," and **sauros**, which means "lizard." These *hadrosaurids* were big, bulky animals.

**Hadrosaurid Skulls**

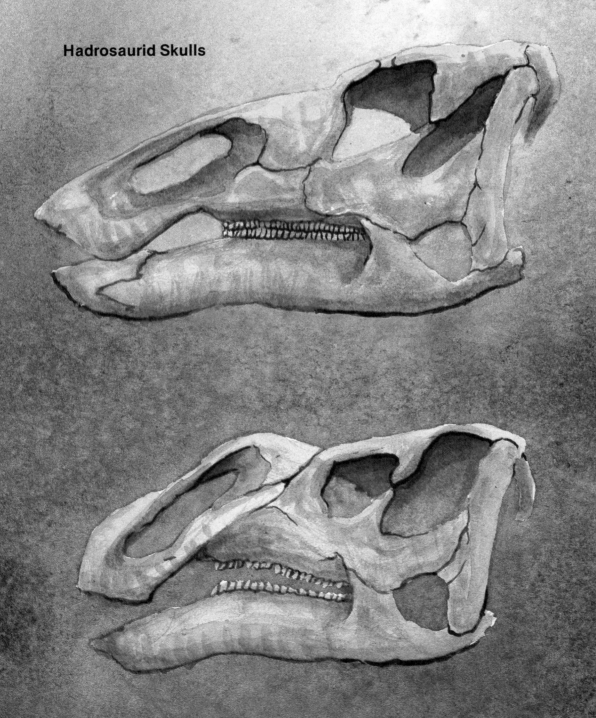

Members of the *hadrosaurid* family had skulls which were broad and flat at the front, like the bill of a duck. Therefore, these animals are often called duckbilled dinosaurs.

However, the shape of the back of the heads on some *hadrosaurids* looked different. In certain members of the *hadrosaurid* family, the back of the heads were flat. Others had heads which were shaped like a dome. Still others had bony crests, which were sometimes hollow.

Scientists still do not know why many of these animals had crests. Perhaps these were decorations that attracted mates. Maybe the crests were lined with cells that detected odors of other animals, which might be enemies. The hollow part of the crest might even have made the sounds dinosaurs made seem louder.

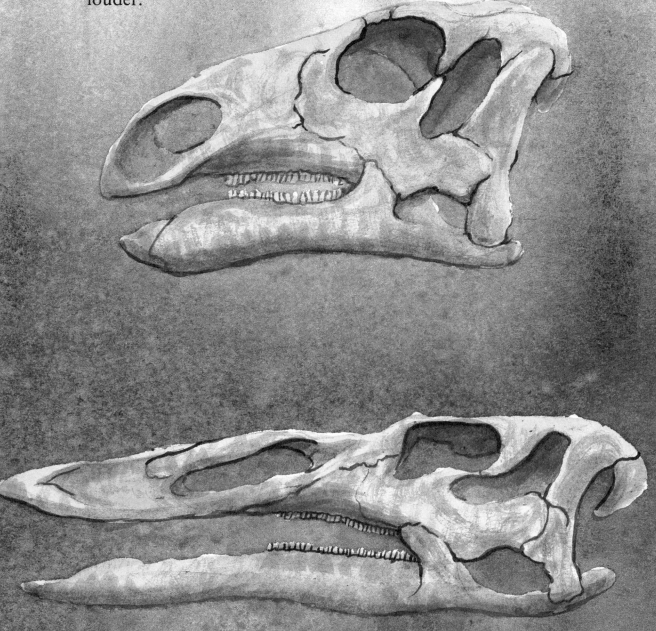

## MAIASAURA ADULTS AND BABIES

The skeleton of the adult *Maiasaura* that Dr. Horner found was about 30 feet (9 m) long and 15 feet (4.6 m) tall. Its bill was short and wide. It had a solid, horn-shaped crest above and between its eyes. This *Maiasaura* would have weighed about 2 tons (1.8 metric tons).

*Maiasaura* walked on two strong, heavy hind legs. There were three toes on the foot of each hind leg. The feet may have been webbed with skin, something like a duck has today.

Each of its short, front legs had four webbed toes. These front legs were not used for walking. However, the webbed toes might have been used as paddles when *Maiasaura* was in the water.

Dr. Horner believed that the newly-hatched *Maiasaura* were about 15 inches (38 cm) long and weighed about 1.5 pounds (3.3 kg). By one month of age, the baby *Maiasaura* were about 3 feet (91 cm) long and 12 inches (30 cm) tall at the hips.

## SWIMMING OR WALKING

Because of their duckbill snouts, scientists used to think that *Maiasaura* dinosaurs spent most of their time in lakes or ponds. Perhaps they could swim to escape an enemy. Powerful tails could have pushed them through the water.

However, most scientists now believe that *Maiasaura* also walked on land. These dinosaurs probably held their bodies horizontally to the ground, with their tails held behind them for balance.

## COLORFUL SKIN

Paleoartists used to think that all dinosaurs had gray, brown, or green skin. Now, scientists know that sometimes animal skin is different colors. The skin of babies might be colored like their surroundings to help them hide from enemies. The color of adults might be in patterns that help them hide, attract a mate, or scare their enemies.

Paleoartists use their imaginations to decide which color to make the skin of *Maiasaura*.

# CHAPTER 3:
# NEW IDEAS ABOUT DINOSAURS

When scientists studied the reports from Dr. Horner, they realized there were many new ideas developing about dinosaurs. For example, it now seemed that dinosaurs cared for their young, that dinosaurs lived in groups, that dinosaurs may have returned to one place every year for nesting and laying eggs, and that young dinosaurs could chew plants.

## CARING FOR BABIES

Scientists used to believe that dinosaurs left their young ones to grow up alone. There is evidence now that this may not be true. In fact, it seems likely that dinosaurs stayed with their young, helped find food for them, and protected them from enemies.

For example, nests of *Maiasaura* have been found that included fossils of young animals of different sizes. This might mean that the babies as well as other young dinosaurs stayed in nests while the parents brought food to them, like today's birds do. Other scientists think the parent dinosaurs led the babies out to eat and then brought them back to the nests.

Teeth of the young dinosaurs were worn smooth, which might show that the babies had been chewing coarse, leafy plants. They might also have eaten leafy plants that had sand on them. This gritty sand may have rubbed on the teeth and helped to make the teeth become smooth.

The adult *Maiasaura* would need to protect its young from other animals which were larger and faster. Such animals might have tried to grab a young Maiasaura from a nest.

## LIVING IN GROUPS

Fossil nests show that groups of fully-grown dinosaurs, along with their young, probably lived together. The fact that many nests of *Maiasaura* were found together means that they would have lived in groups. Each nest was about 6 feet (1.8 m) wide. The nests were separated by the length of one adult *Maiasaura*, which is about 30 feet (9 m). If the adults stayed close to the nests, there would be greater safety for the young *Maiasaura*.

## RETURNING AGAIN

When scientists study the nesting area of *Maiasaura*, they think that these dinosaurs returned to the same spot each year. Here *Maiasaura* would make nests, lay eggs, and raise their young. Dr. Horner has found fossils of nests, eggs, broken eggshells, and the remains of young dinosaurs. These fossils were found in several layers of rock, which might mean that this was used as a nesting area for many years.

Fulton Public Library
Fulton, Illinois

## PLANT-EATERS

Scientists have found evidence that duckbilled dinosaurs, such as *Maiasaura*, ate plants from the land instead of from the water, as was believed earlier. On Egg Mountain, one duckbilled dinosaur was found whose whole body had been fossilized. The stomach contents included twigs, leaves, fruit, pine needles, nuts, and seeds. This fossil stomach did not contain water plants.

*Maiasaura* had no teeth in the front of its jaws. However, the sides of the jaws were lined with hundreds of teeth. Perhaps there were as many as 2,000 teeth arranged in uneven rows. These teeth were good for grinding up tough plants. Fossils show that as one tooth wore out, a new one would grow in its place.

## DINOSAURS DISAPPEARED

Scientists wonder why all these *Maiasaura* dinosaurs died on Egg Mountain. Perhaps an erupting volcano or a mud slide buried them. Perhaps the adult *Maiasaura* died first and the babies had no one to bring them food, so they died, too.

Another question which scientists are studying is the reason for the death of all *Maiasaura,* and other dinosaurs.

There are many different ideas about what caused the death of all dinosaurs. Some scientists think that the air on earth changed. Perhaps many lumps of rock about six miles (10 km) across crashed into earth from space. A cloud of dust from the crash might have caused a change in the weather.

Also, some scientists wonder if a disease or a flood might have killed all the dinosaurs.

Perhaps none of these ideas is correct. No one really knows for sure what killed all the dinosaurs. However, there are no dinosaurs alive today. We can only see fossils and models of dinosaurs in museums.

26

Fulton Public Library
Fulton, Illinois

27

## CONCLUSION: LEARNING TO DRAW DINOSAURS

As the guide finished the tour with Mychal and his family, they returned through the exhibit hall. Here they again saw the paleo-artist, Mr. Henderson. He was drawing more pictures of dinosaurs.

"I've learned a lot about *Maiasaura*," Mychal told Mr. Henderson. "I'd like to draw pictures of *Maiasaura* or other dinosaurs. How should I start?"

"Well, Mychal, people who are interested in dinosaurs can study what paleontologists already know," Mr. Henderson answered.

"You might visit more museums and read books about dinosaurs and other animals," Mr. Henderson continued. "You can learn how to draw plants and trees by visiting greenhouses, walking in the woods, and observing the outdoors. These are things you will need to know in order to make pictures of dinosaurs and how they lived. Now that you have some important information about *Maiasaura*, you probably have some good ideas for a picture of that dinosaur."

"I'd like to buy a book about *Maiasaura* and other dinosaurs," Mychal told his parents. "Then I could read it to learn more about what dinosaurs looked like. Maybe I could even study to become a paleoartist, too, some day."

# MUSEUMS

Now, we can see dinosaurs only in museums. Here are some places where we can see *Maiasaura* fossils today.

**Academy of Natural Sciences,** Philadelphia, PA.

**Museum of the Rockies,** Montana State University, Bozeman, MT.

**Tyrrell Museum of Paleontology,** Drumheller, Alberta (Canada).

# GLOSSARY

**DINOSAUR** (di´ nuh sor´) means "terrible lizard." The Greek word **deinos** means "terrible," and the word **sauros** means "lizard." Dinosaurs, however, were not lizards.

**FOSSILS** (fos´ uhlz) are the remains of plants and animals that lived many years ago. The Latin word **fossilis** means "something dug up."

**HADROSAURID** (had´ ruh sor´ id) is the name of the group of dinosaurs to which Maiasaura belonged. Scientists used the Greek word **hadros,** which means "bulky," and **sauros,** which means "lizard," because they were big, bulky animals. Members of the hadrosaur family looked alike in many ways. The front of their skulls was broad and flat, something like the bill of a duck, so they are sometimes called duckbilled dinosaurs. Some had flat heads, some were dome-shaped, and some had bony crests.

**HYPSILOPHODONTS** (hip si lo´ fuh donts) means "high-crested teeth" because of the high growths on its teeth. The Greek word **hypselos** means "high," the word **lophos** means "crest," and the word **odon** means "tooth." This is the name for a family of dinosaurs which walked on their two hind legs and ate plants. Their teeth were in a single row. They had small heads, short beak-like snouts, large eyes, long legs, and medium-length arms. They ranged from 2.5 to 7 feet (91 cm to 2.1 m) long. Their fossils have been found in North and South America, Europe, and Africa.

**LIZARD** (liz´ uhrd) is a kind of reptile. Most lizards are small with slender, scaly bodies; long tails; and four legs. Dinosaurs were not lizards.

**MAIASAURA** (may ee uh sor´ uh) is from the Greek word **maia** for "good mother" and **saura** for "lizard." Scientists used the feminine word for this animal, because the first adult skull was found near a nest of young.

**MUSEUM** (myoo ze´ uhm) is a place for keeping and exhibiting works of nature and art, scientific objects, and other items.

**PALEOARTIST** (pa´ le o ar´ tist) is a person who makes pictures and models of animals and plants that lived many years ago.

**PALEONTOLOGIST** (pa´ le on tol´ uh jist) is a person who studies fossils to learn about plants and animals from thousands of years ago. The Greek word **palaios** means "ancient," **onta** means "living things," and **logos** means "talking about."

**RESTORATION** (res´ tuh ra´ shun) means making something to be like its original condition. For example, paleoartists make pictures and models of animals and plants that lived many years ago.

**SCIENTIST** (si´ uhn tist) is a person who studies objects or events.

**SKELETON** (skel´ uh tuhn) is the framework of bones of a body.

**THOUSAND** (thou´ zuhnd) is ten times one hundred. It is shown as 1,000.

**TRACKWAYS** (trak´ waz) are paths which are well worn from the feet of animals.

# TIME LINE

**PERIOD** — **CHARACTERISTIC ANIMAL LIFE**

AGE OF THE DINOSAURS

**CRETACEOUS**
65 MILLION YEARS TO 135 MILLION YEARS AGO

Triceratops, Pteranodon, Maiasaura, Tyrannosaurus rex, Plesiosaurus, Ankylosaurus, Seismosaurus

**JURASSIC**
136 MILLION YEARS TO 192 MILLION YEARS AGO

Apatosaurus, Allosaurus, Stegosaurus, Archaeopteryx, Compsognathus

**TRIASSIC**
193 MILLION YEARS TO 224 MILLION YEARS AGO

Mastodonsaurus, Rutiodon, Protosuchus, Plateosaurus

**PERMIAN**
225 MILLION YEARS TO 279 MILLION YEARS AGO

Eryops, Seymouria, Dimetrodon, Titanophoneus

**CARBONIFEROUS**
280 MILLION YEARS TO 345 MILLION YEARS AGO

Urocordylus, Hylonomus, Branchiosaurus